The Illustrated
Book of Hymns and Psalms

Contemplations for every day

Publisher and Creative Director: Nick Wells
Project Editor and Picture Research: Gillian Whitaker
Art Director and Layout Design: Mike Spender
Digital Design and Production: Chris Herbert
Special thanks to Laura Bulbeck and Catherine Taylor

FLAME TREE PUBLISHING
6 Melbray Mews
Fulham, London SW6 3NS
United Kingdom

www.flametreepublishing.com

First published 2016

16 18 20 19 17
1 3 5 7 9 10 8 6 4 2

A CIP record for this book is available from the British Library upon request.

ISBN: 978-1-78361-909-2

Printed in China | Created, Developed & Produced in the United Kingdom

The Illustrated Book of Hymns and Psalms

Contemplations for every day

A special selection edited
by Gillian Whitaker

FLAME TREE
PUBLISHING

Contents

Introduction

ymnody has occupied an important place in the religious and cultural traditions that have developed across societies. This book collates those cherished hymns and psalms that have endured in people's minds, and while the selection predominantly represents Christian practice, it aims to capture the variety of verse that has been repeatedly looked to as a source and channel for comfort, resilience and praise.

Hymns inherently relate to shared experience, ringing out with a voice composed of many voices. In this sense, they fulfil that very human need to feel connected – practisers are linked to those who have sung the same in the past, those who share the present, and those who will sing this common language in the future. Universally recognized images and associations are communicated repeatedly, reinforcing the sense of connection – you will often see in these texts the pilgrim on their journey, the shepherd tending their flock, the ship in a threatening storm, the awesome power of flooding water or light. Taking part in this conversation allows an individual to appreciate their place in something greater than themselves, enabling them to explore and consolidate their relationships – with themselves, their beliefs and God, as well as with others and the world around them.

Bringing together hymns from a range of periods, a spectrum of human emotions can be felt at the heart of this collection, from the unbounded positivity of 'Shine Jesus Shine' to the distress behind 'Abide with Me'. The act of singing or reciting such material is itself a strengthening and restorative exercise: through hymn-singing, beliefs can be both accessed and articulated, and, within this forgiving forum, grievances can be transformed.

Often taking their inspiration direct from scripture, hymns function as songs of praise; psalms also share an etymological link with music. The way in which musical and semantic structures complement one another has helped a great deal in cementing them in religious practice – strong rhythms, logical cadences and repetitive features all contribute a sense of coherency and security to what is being sung. These communal expressions of faith, as such, are able to act as a point of stability in people's lives, helping to navigate what can be at times a complicated and changeable world.

The tradition of hymn-singing demonstrates that hymns and psalms have consistently held an effective role as devotional aids. The four sections of this book aim to cover those familiar hymns and psalms that have been called upon again and again – whether that be the prevailing comfort of Psalm 23 ('The Lord is my shepherd'), the assurance of Psalm 139 ('O Lord, you have searched me out and known me'), the blissful appreciation of 'How Great Thou Art' or the humble voice of 'Amazing Grace'.

Hymns and psalms are fundamentally designed to communicate, and this anthology demonstrates their potency in continuing to do just that, offering us insight into the deep-seated relationship between faith and song that has existed throughout the centuries.

Celebration & Gratitude

All People That on Earth Do Dwell

William Kethe (d. 1594)

All people that on earth do dwell,
sing to the Lord with cheerful voice:
him serve with mirth, his praise forth tell,
come ye before him and rejoice.

The Lord, ye know, is God indeed;
without our aid he did us make:
we are his folk, he doth us feed,
and for his sheep he doth us take.

O enter then his gates with praise,
approach with joy his courts unto;
praise, laud, and bless his Name always,
for it is seemly so to do.

For why? the Lord our God is good,
his mercy is for ever sure;
his truth at all times firmly stood,
and shall from age to age endure.

To Father, Son, and Holy Ghost,
the God whom heaven and earth adore,
from men and from the angel host
be praise and glory evermore.

God of Mercy, God of Grace
Henry Francis Lyte (1793 – 1847)

God of mercy, God of grace,
show the brightness of thy face.
Shine upon us, Saviour, shine,
fill thy Church with light divine,
and thy saving health extend
unto earth's remotest end.

Let the people praise thee, Lord;
be by all that live adored.
Let the nations shout and sing
glory to their Saviour King;
at thy feet their tribute pay,
and thy holy will obey.

Let the people praise thee, Lord;
earth shall then her fruits afford;
God to man his blessing give,
man to God devoted live;
all below, and all above,
one in joy, and light, and love.

When I Survey the Wondrous Cross
Isaac Watts (1674–1748)

When I survey the wondrous cross
where the young Prince of Glory died,
my richest gain I count but loss,
and pour contempt on all my pride.

Forbid it, Lord, that I should boast,
save in the cross of Christ, my God:
all the vain things that charm me most,
I sacrifice them to his blood.

See, from his head, his hands, his feet,
sorrow and love flow mingled down!
Did e'er such love and sorrow meet,
or thorns compose so rich a crown?

Were the whole realm of nature mine,
that were an offering far too small;
love so amazing, so divine,
demands my soul, my life, my all.

We Plough the Fields, and Scatter

Matthias Claudius (1740–1815); trans. Jane Montgomery Campbell (1817–78)

We plough the fields, and scatter
the good seed on the land,
but it is fed and watered
by God's almighty hand;
he sends the snow in winter,
the warmth to swell the grain,
the breezes and the sunshine,
and soft refreshing rain.

All good gifts around us
are sent from heaven above,
then thank the Lord, O thank the Lord
for all his love.

He only is the Maker
of all things near and far;
he paints the wayside flower,
he lights the evening star;
the winds and waves obey him,
by him the birds are fed;
much more to us, his children,
he gives our daily bread. *Refrain*

We thank thee, then, O Father,
for all things bright and good,
the seed time and the harvest,
our life, our health, and food;
no gifts have we to offer,
for all thy love imparts,
and, what thou most desirest,
our humble, thankful hearts. *Refrain*

Be Still for the Presence of the Lord
David J. Evans (b. 1957)

Be still, for the presence of the Lord,

The Holy One is here;

Come bow before Him now

With reverence and fear

In Him no sin is found

We stand on holy ground.

Be still, for the presence of the Lord,

The Holy One is here.

Be still, for the glory of the Lord

Is shining all around

He burns with holy fire,

With splendour He is crowned

How awesome is the sight

Our radiant King of light!

Be still, for the glory of the Lord

Is shining all around.

Be still, for the power of the Lord

Is moving in this place:

He comes to cleanse and heal,

To minister His grace –

No work too hard for Him.

In faith receive from Him.

Be still, for the power of the Lord

Is moving in this place.

Psalm 136: 1-4, 23-26

O give thanks to the Lord, for he is good.
for his mercy endures for ever.
O give thanks to the God of gods.
for his mercy endures for ever.
O give thanks to the Lord of lords.
for his mercy endures for ever.
To him who alone does great wonders.
for his mercy endures for ever.

Who remembered us in our humiliation.
for his mercy endures for ever.
And delivered us from our enemies.
for his mercy endures for ever.
Who gives food to all that lives.
for his mercy endures for ever.
O give thanks to the God of heaven.
for his mercy endures for ever.

How Great Thou Art
Stuart K. Hine (1899–1989)

O Lord my God! when I in awesome wonder
Consider all the works Thy hand hath made,
I see the stars, I hear the mighty thunder,
Thy power throughout the universe displayed:

Then sings my soul, my Saviour God to Thee,
How great Thou art! How great Thou art!
Then sings my soul, my Saviour God, to Thee,
How great Thou art! How great Thou art!

When through the woods and forest glades I wander
And hear the birds sing sweetly in the trees;
When I look down from lofty mountain grandeur,
And hear the brook, and feel the gentle breeze; *Refrain*

And when I think that God His Son not sparing,
Sent Him to die – I scarce can take it in.
That on the cross my burden gladly bearing,
He bled and died to take away my sin: *Refrain*

When Christ shall come with shout of acclamation
And take me home – what joy shall fill my heart!
Then shall I bow in humble adoration
And there proclaim, my God, how great Thou art! *Refrain*

For the Beauty of the Earth
Folliott Sandford Pierpoint (1835–1917)

For the beauty of the earth,
for the beauty of the skies,
for the love which from our birth
over and around us lies

Christ our God, to thee we raise
this our sacrifice of praise.

For the beauty of each hour
of the day and of the night,
hill and vale, and tree and flower,
sun and moon, and stars of light, *Refrain*

For the joy of ear and eye,
for the heart and brain's delight,
for the mystic harmony
linking sense to sound and sight, *Refrain*

For the joy of human love,
brother, sister, parent, child,
friends on earth, and friends above,
for all gentle thoughts and mild, *Refrain*

For each perfect gift of thine
to our race so freely given,
graces human and divine,
flowers of earth and buds of heaven, *Refrain*

For thy Bride that evermore
lifteth holy hands above,
offering up on every shore
this pure sacrifice of love, *Refrain*

For the martyrs' crown of light,
for thy prophets' eagle eye,
for thy bold confessors' might,
for the lips of infancy, *Refrain*

For thy virgins' robes of snow,
for thy maiden Mother mild,
for thyself, with hearts aglow,
Jesus, Victim undefiled, *Refrain*

And Can It Be That I Should Gain?

Charles Wesley (1707–88)

And can it be that I should gain
An interest in the Saviour's blood?
Died He for me, who caused His pain –
For me, who Him to death pursued?
Amazing love! How can it be,
That Thou, my God, shouldst die for me?
Amazing love! How can it be,
That Thou, my God, shouldst die for me?

'Tis mystery all: th'Immortal dies:
Who can explore His strange design?
In vain the firstborn seraph tries
To sound the depths of love divine.
'Tis mercy all! Let earth adore,
Let angel minds inquire no more.
'Tis mercy all! Let earth adore;
Let angel minds inquire no more.

He left His Father's throne above
So free, so infinite His grace –
Emptied Himself of all but love,
And bled for Adam's helpless race:
'Tis mercy all, immense and free,
For O my God, it found out me!
'Tis mercy all, immense and free,
For O my God, it found out me!

Long my imprisoned spirit lay,
Fast bound in sin and nature's night;
Thine eye diffused a quickening ray —
I woke, the dungeon flamed with light;
My chains fell off, my heart was free,
I rose, went forth, and followed Thee.
My chains fell off, my heart was free,
I rose, went forth, and followed Thee.

Still the small inward voice I hear,
That whispers all my sins forgiven;
Still the atoning blood is near,
That quenched the wrath of hostile Heaven.
I feel the life His wounds impart;
I feel the Saviour in my heart.
I feel the life His wounds impart;
I feel the Saviour in my heart.

No condemnation now I dread;
Jesus, and all in Him, is mine;
Alive in Him, my living Head,
And clothed in righteousness divine,
Bold I approach th'eternal throne,
And claim the crown, through Christ my own.
Bold I approach th'eternal throne,
And claim the crown, through Christ my own.

Psalm 8: 3–9
Attr. King David (c. 1040 bc–970 bc)

When I consider your heavens,
   the work of your fingers,
the moon and the stars,
   which you have set in order,
What is man, that you should be mindful of him,
   or the son of man, that you should care for him?

Yet you have made him little less than a god,
   and have crowned him with glory and honour.
You have made him the master of your handiwork,
   and have put all things in subjection beneath his feet,
All sheep and oxen,
   and all the creatures of the field,
The birds of the air,
   and the fish of the sea,
and everything that moves in the pathways of the great waters.

O Lord our Governor,
   how glorious is your name in all the earth!

Holy, Holy, Holy!
Reginald Heber (1783–1928)

Holy, holy, holy! Lord God Almighty!
Early in the morning our song shall rise to thee.
Holy, holy, holy! Merciful and mighty,
God in three Persons, blessèd Trinity.

Holy, holy, holy! All saints adore thee,
casting down their golden crowns around the glassy sea;
cherubim and seraphim falling down before thee,
which wert, and art, and evermore shalt be.

Holy, holy, holy! Though the darkness hide thee,
though the sinful human eye thy glory may not see,
only thou art holy; there is none beside thee,
perfect in power, in love, and purity.

Holy, holy, holy! Lord God Almighty!
All thy works shall praise thy Name, in earth, and sky, and sea;
Holy, holy, holy! Merciful and mighty,
God in three Persons, blessèd Trinity.

Praise, My Soul, the King of Heaven
Henry Francis Lyte (1793–1847)

Praise, my soul, the King of heaven;
to his feet thy tribute bring;
ransomed, healed, restored, forgiven,
evermore his praises sing:
Alleluia, alleluia! Praise the everlasting King.

Praise him for his grace and favor
to our fathers in distress;
praise him still the same for ever,
slow to chide and swift to bless:
Alleluia, alleluia! Glorious in his faithfulness.

Father-like, he tends and spares us;
well our feeble frame he knows;
in his hand he gently bears us,
rescues us from all our foes.
Alleluia, alleluia! Widely yet his mercy flows.

Angels, help us to adore him;
ye behold him face to face;
sun and moon, bow down before him,
dwellers all in time and space.
Alleluia, alleluia! Praise with us the God of grace.

Blessed Assurance
Fanny Crosby (1820–1915)

Blessèd assurance, Jesus is mine:
O what a foretaste of glory divine!
Heir of salvation purchase of God;
born of his Spirit, washed in his blood:

This is my story, this is my song,
praising my Saviour, all the day long.

Perfect submission, perfect delight,
visions of rapture burst on my sight;
angels descending bring from above
echoes of mercy, whispers of love: *Refrain*

Perfect submission, all is at rest,
I in my Saviour am happy and blest;
watching and waiting, looking above,
filled with his goodness, lost in his love. *Refrain*

All Things Bright and Beautiful
Cecil Frances Alexander (d. 1895)

All things bright and beautiful,
all creatures great and small,
all things wise and wonderful,
the Lord God made them all.

Each little flower that opens,
each little bird that sings,
he made their glowing colours,
he made their tiny wings. *Refrain*

The purple-headed mountain,
the river running by,
the sunset, and the morning
that brightens up the sky. *Refrain*

The cold wind in the winter,
the pleasant summer sun,
the ripe fruits in the garden,
he made them every one. *Refrain*

He gave us eyes to see them,
and lips that we might tell
how great is God Almighty,
who has made all things well. *Refrain*

Give Me Joy in My Heart
(Traditional)

Give me joy in my heart, keep me praising,
Give me joy in my heart, I pray,
Give me joy in my heart, keep me praising,
Keep me praising 'til the break of day.

Sing hosanna, sing hosanna,
Sing hosanna to the King of kings!
Sing hosanna, sing hosanna,
Sing hosanna to the King.

Give me peace in my heart, keep me praying,
Give me peace in my heart, I pray,
Give me peace in my heart, keep me praying,
Keep me praying 'til the end of day. *Refrain*

Give me love in my heart, keep me praising,
Give me love in my heart, I pray,
Give me love in my heart, keep me praising,
Keep me praising 'til the break of day. *Refrain*

Give my oil in my lamp, keep me burning,
Give me oil in my lamp, I pray,
Give my oil in my lamp, keep me burning,
Keep me burning 'til the end of day. *Refrain*

The King of Love My Shepherd Is
Henry Williams Baker (1821–77)

The King of love my shepherd is,
whose goodness faileth never;
I nothing lack if I am his,
and he is mine for ever.

Where streams of living water flow,
my ransomed soul he leadeth,
and where the verdant pastures grow,
with food celestial feedeth.

Perverse and foolish oft I strayed,
but yet in love He sought me,
and on his shoulder gently laid,
and home, rejoicing, brought me.

In death's dark vale I fear no ill
with thee, dear Lord, beside me;
thy rod and staff my comfort still,
thy cross before to guide me.

Thou spread'st a table in my sight;
thy unction grace bestoweth;
and O what transport of delight
from thy pure chalice floweth!

And so through all the length of days
thy goodness faileth never:
Good Shepherd, may I sing thy praise
within thy house for ever.

In the Bleak Midwinter (1872)
Christina Rossetti (1830–94)

In the bleak midwinter, frosty wind made moan,
Earth stood hard as iron, water like a stone;
Snow had fallen, snow on snow, snow on snow,
In the bleak midwinter, long ago.

Our God, Heaven cannot hold Him, nor earth sustain;
Heaven and earth shall flee away when He comes to reign.
In the bleak midwinter a stable place sufficed
The Lord God Almighty, Jesus Christ.

Enough for Him, whom cherubim, worship night and day,
Breastful of milk, and a mangerful of hay;
Enough for Him, whom angels fall before,
The ox and ass and camel which adore.

Angels and archangels may have gathered there,
Cherubim and seraphim thronged the air;
But His mother only, in her maiden bliss,
Worshipped the beloved with a kiss.

What can I give Him, poor as I am?
If I were a shepherd, I would bring a lamb;
If I were a Wise Man, I would do my part;
Yet what I can I give Him: give my heart.

Love Came Down at Christmas
Christina Rossetti (1830–94)

Love came down at Christmas,
love all lovely, love divine;
love was born at Christmas:
star and angels gave the sign.

Worship we the Godhead,
love incarnate, love divine;
worship we our Jesus,
but wherewith the sacred sign?

Love shall be our token;
love be yours and love be mine,
Love to God and to all men,
love for plea and gift and sign.

Guidance & Inspiration

Guide Me O Thou Great Redeemer

William Williams (1717–91);
trans. Peter Williams (1723–96)

Guide me, O thou great Redeemer,
pilgrim through this barren land;
I am weak, but thou art mighty;
hold me with thy powerful hand;
Bread of heaven,
feed me now and evermore.

Open now the crystal fountain,
whence the healing stream doth flow;
let the fiery cloudy pillar
lead me all my journey through;
strong Deliverer,
be thou still my Strength and Shield.

When I tread the verge of Jordan,
bid my anxious fears subside;
bear me through the swelling current,
land me safe on Canaan's side;
songs of praises,
I will ever give to thee.

Through All the Changing Scenes of Life
Nahum Tate (1652–1715) and Nicholas Brady (1659–1726)

Through all the changing scenes of life,
in trouble and in joy,
the praises of my God shall still
my heart and tongue employ.

O magnify the Lord with me,
with me exalt his Name;
when in distress to him I called,
he to my rescue came.

The hosts of God encamp around
the dwellings of the just;
deliverance he affords to all
who on his succour trust.

O make but trial of his love;
experience will decide
how blest are they, and only they
who in his truth confide.

Fear him, ye saints, and you will then
have nothing else to fear;
make you his service your delight;
your wants shall be his care.

For God preserves the souls of those
who on his truth depend;
to them and their posterity
his blessing shall descend.

Psalm 1: 1-3

Blessed is the man
  who has not walked in the counsel of the ungodly
nor followed the way of sinners,
  nor taken his seat amongst the scornful.
But his delight is in the law of the Lord,
  and on that law will he ponder day and night.

He is like a tree planted beside streams of water,
  that yields its fruit in due season.
Its leaves also shall not wither;
  and look, whatever he does, it shall prosper.

Awake, My Soul, and with the Sun
(Selection of Verses)
Thomas Ken (1637–1711)

Awake, my soul, and with the sun
Thy daily stage of duty run;
Shake off dull sloth, and joyful rise,
To pay thy morning sacrifice.

By influence of the Light divine
Let thy own light to others shine.
Reflect all Heaven's propitious ways
In ardent love, and cheerful praise.

Lord, I my vows to Thee renew;
Disperse my sins as morning dew.
Guard my first springs of thought and will,
And with Thyself my spirit fill.

Direct, control, suggest, this day,
All I design, or do, or say,
That all my powers, with all their might,
In Thy sole glory may unite.

Praise God, from Whom all blessings flow;
Praise Him, all creatures here below;
Praise Him above, ye heavenly host;
Praise Father, Son, and Holy Ghost.

Lead, Kindly Light
John Henry Newman (1801–90)

Lead, kindly Light, amid th'encircling gloom,
lead thou me on!
The night is dark, and I am far from home;
lead thou me on!
Keep thou my feet; I do not ask to see
the distant scene; one step enough for me.

I was not ever thus, nor prayed that thou
shouldst lead me on;
I loved to choose and see my path; but now
lead thou me on!
I loved the garish day, and, spite of fears,
pride ruled my will: remember not past years!

So long thy power hath blessed me, sure it still
will lead me on.
O'er moor and fen, o'er crag and torrent, till
the night is gone,
And with the morn those angel faces smile,
which I have loved long since, and lost awhile!

*P*salm 91: 1-6, 14-16

He who dwells in the shelter of the Most High
    who abides under the shadow of the Almighty,
He will say to the Lord 'You are my refuge and my stronghold,
    my God in whom I trust.'
For he will deliver you from the snare of the hunter
    and from the destroying curse.
He will cover you with his wings,
    and you will be safe under his feathers;
    his faithfulness will be your shield and defence.
You shall not be afraid of any terror by night,
    or of the arrow that flies by day,
    of the pestilence that walks about in darkness,
    or the plague that destroys at noonday.

'He has set his love upon me,
    and therefore I will deliver him;
I will lift him out of danger,
    because he has known my name.
'When he calls upon me I will answer him;
    I will be with him in trouble,
    I will rescue him and bring him to honour.
'With long life I will satisfy him
    and fill him with my salvation.'

It Is Well with My Soul
Horatio G. Spafford (1828–88)

When peace, like a river, attendeth my way,
When sorrows like sea billows roll;
Whatever my lot, Thou has taught me to say,
It is well, it is well, with my soul.

It is well, with my soul,
It is well, with my soul,
It is well, it is well, with my soul.

Though Satan should buffet, though trials should come,
Let this blest assurance control,
That Christ has regarded my helpless estate,
And hath shed His own blood for my soul. *Refrain*

My sin, oh, the bliss of this glorious thought!
My sin, not in part but the whole,
Is nailed to the cross, and I bear it no more,
Praise the Lord, praise the Lord, O my soul! *Refrain*

For me, be it Christ, be it Christ hence to live:
If Jordan above me shall roll,
No pang shall be mine, for in death as in life
Thou wilt whisper Thy peace to my soul. *Refrain*

But, Lord, 'tis for Thee, for Thy coming we wait,

The sky, not the grave, is our goal;

Oh trump of the angel! Oh voice of the Lord!

Blessèd hope, blessèd rest of my soul! *Refrain*

And Lord, haste the day when my faith shall be sight,

The clouds be rolled back as a scroll;

The trump shall resound, and the Lord shall descend,

Even so, it is well with my soul. *Refrain*

I Will Go in the Strength of the Lord

Edward Turney (1816–72)

I will go in the strength of the Lord,

In the path He hath marked for my feet:

I will follow the light of His Word,

Nor shrink from the dangers I meet.

His presence my steps shall attend:

His fullness my wants shall supply;

On Him, till my journey shall end,

My hope shall securely rely.

I will go in the strength of the Lord,

To the work He appoints me to do:

In the joy which His smile shall afford

My soul shall her vigour renew.

His wisdom will guard me from harm,

His pow'r my sufficiency prove;

I will trust His omnipotent arm,

I will rest in His covenant love.

I will go in the strength of the Lord,

To each conflict which faith may require,

His grace, as my shield and reward,

My courage and zeal shall inspire.

If He issue the word of command

To meet and encounter the foe,

Though with sling and with stone in my hand,

In the strength of the Lord I will go.

Come, Holy Ghost, Our Souls Inspire
Trans. John Cosin (1594–1672)

Come, Holy Ghost, our souls inspire,
and lighten with celestial fire.
Thou the anointing Spirit art,
who dost thy sevenfold gifts impart.

Thy blessed unction from above
is comfort, life, and fire of love.
Enable with perpetual light
the dullness of our blinded sight.

Anoint and cheer our soiled face
with the abundance of thy grace.
Keep far from foes, give peace at home:
where thou art guide, no ill can come.

Teach us to know the Father, Son,
and thee, of both, to be but One,
that through the ages all along,
this may be our endless song:

Praise to thy eternal merit,
Father, Son, and Holy Spirit.

Psalm 139: 1-12, 23-24
Attr. King David (c. 1040 bc–970 bc)

O Lord, you have searched me out and known me:
    you know when I sit or when I stand,
    you comprehend my thoughts long before.
You discern my path and the places where I rest;
    you are acquainted with all my ways.
For there is not a word on my tongue
    but you, Lord, know it altogether.
You have encompassed me behind and before,
    and have laid your hand upon me.
Such knowledge is too wonderful for me,
    so high that I cannot endure it.
Where shall I go from your spirit,
    or where shall I flee from your presence?
If I ascend into heaven you are there;
    if I make my bed in the grave you are there also.
If I spread out my wings towards the morning,
    or dwell in the uttermost parts of the sea,
Even there your hand shall lead me:
    and your right hand shall hold me.
If I say 'Surely the darkness will cover me,
    and the night will enclose me',
The darkness is no darkness with you,
    but the night is as clear as the day;
    the darkness and the light are both alike.

For you have created my inward parts;
    you knit me together in my mother's womb.
I will praise you, for you are to be feared;
    fearful are your acts, and wonderful your works.
You knew my soul,
    and my bones were not hidden from you
 when I was formed in secret,
    and woven in the depths of the earth.
Your eyes saw my limbs when they were yet imperfect,
    and in your book were all my members written;
Day by day they were fashioned,
    and not one was late in growing.
How deep are your thoughts to me, O God,
    and how great is the sum of them!
Were I to count them,
    they are more in number than the sand;
    were I to come to the end, I would still be with you.

Search me out, O God, and know my heart;
    put me to the proof and know my thoughts.
Look well lest there be any way of wickedness in me,
    and lead me in the way that is everlasting.

Psalm 84: 1-4, 10-12

How lovely is your dwelling-place,
  O Lord God of hosts!
My soul has a desire and longing to enter the courts of the Lord;
  my heart and my flesh rejoice in the living God.
The sparrow has found her a home,
  and the swallow a nest where she may lay her young:
  even your altar, O Lord of hosts, my King and my God.
Blessed are those who dwell in your house;
  they will always be praising you.

One day in your courts is better than a thousand;
  I would rather stand at the threshold of the house of my God
  than dwell in the tents of ungodliness.
For the Lord God is a rampart and a shield,
  the Lord gives favour and honour,
  and no good thing will he withhold
  from those who walk in innocence.

O Lord God of hosts,
  blessed is the man who puts his trust in you.

My Soul, There Is a Country
Henry Vaughan (1621–95)

My soul, there is a country
far beyond the stars,
where stands a winged sentry
all skillful in the wars:

there above noise, and danger,
sweet peace sits crowned with smiles,
and One born in a manger
commands the beauteous files.

He is thy gracious Friend,
and – O my soul, awake!
did in pure love descend,
to die here for thy sake.

If thou canst get but thither,
there grows the flower of peace,
the Rose that cannot wither,
thy fortress and thy ease.

Leave then thy foolish ranges,
for none can thee secure
but one who never changes,
thy God, thy life, thy cure.

He Who Would Valiant Be

John Bunyan, 1684 (1628–88)
modified by Percy Dearmer (1867–1936)

He who would valiant be 'gainst all disaster,
let him in constancy follow the Master.
There's no discouragement shall make him once relent
his first avowed intent to be a pilgrim.

Who so beset him round with dismal stories
do but themselves confound his strength the more is.
No foes shall stay his might; though he with giants fight,
he will make good his right to be a pilgrim.

Since, Lord, thou dost defend us with thy Spirit,
We know we at the end, shall life inherit.
Then fancies flee away! I'll fear not what men say,
I'll labour night and day to be a pilgrim.

O Love That Wilt Not Let Me Go
George Matheson (1842–1906)

O Love that wilt not let me go,
I rest my weary soul in thee;
I give thee back the life I owe,
that in thine ocean depths its flow
may richer, fuller be.

O Light that followest all my way,
I yield my flickering torch to thee;
my heart restores its borrowed ray,
that in thy sunshine's blaze its day
may brighter, fairer be.

O Joy that seekest me through pain,
I cannot close my heart to thee;
I trace the rainbow through the rain,
and feel the promise is not vain,
that morn shall tearless be.

O Cross that liftest up my head,
I dare not ask to fly from thee;
I lay in dust life's glory dead,
and from the ground there blossoms red
life that shall endless be.

All My Hope on God is Founded
Joachim Neander (1650–80),
trans. Robert Bridges (1844–1930)

All my hope on God is founded;
he doth still my trust renew,
me through change and chance he guideth,
only good and only true.
God unknown, he alone
calls my heart to be his own.

Pride of man and earthly glory,
sword and crown betray his trust;
what with care and toil he buildeth,
tower and temple fall to dust.
But God's power, hour by hour,
is my temple and my tower.

God's great goodness aye endureth,
deep his wisdom, passing thought:
splendour, light and life attend him,
beauty springeth out of naught.
Evermore from his store
newborn worlds rise and adore.

Daily doth the almighty Giver
bounteous gifts on us bestow;
his desire our soul delighteth,
pleasure leads us where we go.
Love doth stand at his hand;
joy doth wait on his command.

Still from man to God eternal
sacrifice of praise be done,
high above all praises praising
for the gift of Christ, his Son.
Christ doth call one and all:
ye who follow shall not fall.

The Day Thou Gavest, Lord, Is Ended

John Ellerton (1826–93)

The day thou gavest, Lord, is ended,
the darkness falls at thy behest;
to thee our morning hymns ascended,
thy praise shall sanctify our rest.

We thank thee that thy Church, unsleeping
while earth rolls onward into light,
through all the world her watch is keeping
and rests not now by day nor night.

As o'er each continent and island
the dawn leads on another day,
the voice of prayer is never silent,
nor dies the strain of praise away.

The sun that bids us rest is waking
our brethren 'neath the western sky,
and hour by hour fresh lips are making
thy wondrous doings heard on high.

So be it, Lord; thy throne shall never,
like earth's proud empires, pass away;
thy kingdom stands, and grows for ever,
till all thy creatures own thy sway.

Psalm 23
Attr. King David (c. 1040 bc–970 bc)

The Lord is my shepherd,
   therefore can I lack nothing.
He will make me lie down in green pastures,
   and lead me beside still waters.
He will refresh my soul,
   and guide me in right pathways for his name's sake.
Though I walk through the valley of the shadow of death,
   I will fear no evil,
 for you are with me, your rod and your staff comfort me.
You spread a table before me
   in the face of those who trouble me;
   you have anointed my head with oil, and my cup will be full.
Surely your goodness and loving-kindness
   will follow me all the days of my life,
 and I shall dwell in the house of the Lord for ever.

I Danced in the Morning (Lord of the Dance)

Sydney Carter (1915–2004)

I danced in the morning
When the world was begun,
And I danced in the moon
And the stars and the sun,
And I came down from heaven
And I danced on the earth,
At Bethlehem
I had my birth.

Dance, then, wherever you may be,
I am the Lord of the Dance, said he,
And I'll lead you all, wherever you may be,
And I'll lead you all in the Dance, said he.

I danced for the scribe
And the pharisee,
But they would not dance
And they wouldn't follow me.
I danced for the fishermen,
For James and John –
They came with me
And the Dance went on. *Refrain*

I danced on the Sabbath
And I cured the lame;
The holy people
Said it was a shame.
They whipped and they stripped
And they hung me on high,
And they left me there
On a Cross to die. *Refrain*

I danced on a Friday
When the sky turned black –
It's hard to dance
With the devil on your back.
They buried my body
And they thought I'd gone,
But I am the Dance,
And I still go on. *Refrain*

They cut me down
And I leapt up high;
I am the life
That'll never, never die;
I'll live in you
If you'll live in me –
I am the Lord
Of the Dance, said he. *Refrain*

Supplication & Salvation

Amazing Grace
John Newton (1725–1807)
with final verse attributed to John P. Rees (1828–1900)

Amazing grace! how sweet the sound,
that saved a wretch like me!
I once was lost but now am found,
was blind but now I see.

'Twas grace that taught my heart to fear,
and grace my fears relieved;
how precious did that grace appear
the hour I first believed!

The Lord has promised good to me,
his word my hope secures;
he will my shield and portion be
as long as life endures.

Through many dangers, toils, and snares,
I have already come;
'tis grace hath brought me safe thus far,
and grace will lead me home.

Yea, when this flesh and heart shall fail,
And mortal life shall cease,
I shall possess, within the veil,
A life of joy and peace.

The world shall soon dissolve like snow,
The sun refuse to shine;
But God, who called me here below,
Shall be forever mine.

When we've been there ten thousand years,
bright shining as the sun,
we've no less days to sing God's praise
than when we'd first begun.

Psalm 40: 1-3, 11-12
Attr. King David (c. 1040 bc–970 bc)

I waited patiently for the Lord,
 and he inclined to me and heard my cry.
He brought me up from the pit of roaring waters,
 out of the mire and clay,
 and set my feet upon a rock, and made firm my foothold.
And he has put a new song in my mouth,
 even a song of thanksgiving to our God.
Many shall see it and fear,
 and shall put their trust in the Lord.

O Lord, do not withhold your mercy from me;
 let your loving-kindness and your truth ever preserve me.
For innumerable troubles have come upon me;
 my sins have overtaken me, and I cannot see.
They are more in number than the hairs of my head,
 therefore my heart fails me.
Be pleased, O Lord, to deliver me;
 O Lord, make haste to help me.

New Every Morning Is the Love

John Keble (1792–1866)

New every morning is the love
our wakening and uprising prove;
through sleep and darkness safely brought,
restored to life and power and thought.

New mercies, each returning day,
hover around us while we pray;
new perils past, new sins forgiven,
new thoughts of God, new hopes of heaven.

If on our daily course our mind
be set to hallow all we find,
new treasures still, of countless price,
God will provide for sacrifice.

Old friends, old scenes, will lovelier be,
as more of heaven in each we see;
some softening gleam of love and prayer
shall dawn on every cross and care.

The trivial round, the common task,
will furnish all we ought to ask:
room to deny ourselves; a road
to bring us daily nearer God.

Only, O Lord, in thy dear love,
fit us for perfect rest above;
and help us, this and every day,
to live more nearly as we pray.

What a Friend We Have in Jesus

Joseph Scriven (1819–86)

What a Friend we have in Jesus,
all our sins and griefs to bear!
What a privilege to carry
everything to God in prayer!
O what peace we often forfeit,
O what needless pain we bear,
all because we do not carry
everything to God in prayer.

Have we trials and temptations?
Is there trouble anywhere?
We should never be discouraged;
take it to the Lord in prayer.
Can we find a friend so faithful
who will all our sorrows share?
Jesus knows our every weakness;
take it to the Lord in prayer.

Are we weak and heavy laden,
cumbered with a load of care?
Precious Saviour, still our refuge,
take it to the Lord in prayer.
Do your friends despise, forsake you?
Take it to the Lord in prayer!
In his arms he'll take and shield you;
you will find a solace there.

Blessed Saviour, thou hast promised
thou wilt all our burdens bear
may we ever, Lord, be bringing all
to thee in earnest prayer.
Soon in glory bright unclouded there
will be no need for prayer
Rapture, praise and endless worship
will be our sweet portion there.

Eternal Father, Strong to Save
William Whiting (1825–78)

Eternal Father, strong to save,
whose arm hath bound the restless wave,
who bidd'st the mighty ocean deep
its own appointed limits keep:
O hear us when we cry to thee
for those in peril on the sea.

O Christ, whose voice the waters heard
and hushed their raging at thy word,
who walkedst on the foaming deep,
and calm amid the storm didst sleep;
O hear us when we cry to thee
for those in peril on the sea.

Most Holy Spirit, who didst brood
upon the chaos dark and rude,
and bid its angry tumult cease,
and give, for wild confusion, peace:
O hear us when we cry to thee
for those in peril on the sea.

O Trinity of love and power,
our brethren shield in danger's hour;
from rock and tempest, fire and foe,
protect them wheresoe'er they go;
thus evermore shall rise to thee
glad hymns of praise from land and sea.

Psalm 42: 1-3, 9-11

As a deer longs for the running brooks,
    so longs my soul for you, O God.
My soul is thirsty for God, thirsty for the living God;
    when shall I come and see his face?
My tears have been my food day and night,
    while they ask me all day long 'Where now is your God?'

I will say to God, my rock, 'Why have you forgotten me;
    why must I go like a mourner because the enemy oppresses me?'
Like a sword through my bones, my enemies have mocked me,
    while they ask me all day long 'Where now is your God?'
Why are you so full of heaviness, my soul,
    and why so unquiet within me?
O put your trust in God,
    for I will praise him yet, who is my deliverer and my God.

Psalm 43

Give judgement for me, O God,
   take up my cause against an ungodly people.
 Deliver me from deceitful and wicked men.
For you are God my refuge;
   why have you turned me away?
   why must I go like a mourner because the enemy oppresses me?
O send out your light and your truth, and let them lead me;
   let them guide me to your holy hill and to your dwelling.
Then I shall go to the altar of God,
   to God my joy and my delight,
   and to the harp I shall sing your praises,
   O God, my God.
Why are you so full of heaviness, my soul,
   and why so unquiet within me?
O put your trust in God,
   for I will praise him yet, who is my deliverer and my God.

Love Divine, All Loves Excelling

Charles Wesley (1707–88)

Love divine, all loves excelling,
Joy of heaven to earth come down;
Fix in us thy humble dwelling;
All thy faithful mercies crown!
Jesus, Thou art all compassion,
Pure unbounded love Thou art;
Visit us with Thy salvation;
Enter every trembling heart.

Breathe, O breathe Thy loving Spirit,
Into every troubled breast!
Let us all in Thee inherit;
Let us find that second rest.
Take away our bent to sinning;
Alpha and Omega be;
End of faith, as its Beginning,
Set our hearts at liberty.

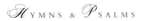

Come, Almighty to deliver,
Let us all Thy life receive;
Suddenly return and never,
Never more Thy temples leave.
Thee we would be always blessing,
Serve Thee as Thy hosts above,
Pray and praise Thee without ceasing,
Glory in Thy perfect love.

Finish, then, Thy new creation;
Pure and spotless let us be.
Let us see Thy great salvation
Perfectly restored in Thee;
Changed from glory into glory,
Till in heaven we take our place,
Till we cast our crowns before Thee,
Lost in wonder, love, and praise.

Immortal, Invisible, God Only Wise
Walter Chalmers Smith (1824–1908)

Immortal, invisible, God only wise,
in light inaccessible hid from our eyes,
most blessed, most glorious, the Ancient of Days,
almighty, victorious, thy great Name we praise.

Unresting, unhasting, and silent as light,
nor wanting, nor wasting, thou rulest in might;
thy justice like mountains high soaring above
thy clouds, which are fountains of goodness and love.

To all life thou givest, to both great and small;
in all life thou livest, the true life of all;
we blossom and flourish, like leaves on the tree,
then wither and perish; but nought changeth thee.

Great Father of glory, pure Father of light,
thine angels adore thee, all veiling their sight;
all laud we would render: O help us to see
'tis only the splendour of light hideth thee.

Just as I Am (1841)
Charlotte Elliott (1789–1871)

Just as I am, without one plea,
but that thy blood was shed for me,
and that thou bidd'st me come to thee,
O Lamb of God, I come, I come.

Just as I am, and waiting not
to rid my soul of one dark blot,
to thee, whose blood can cleanse each spot,
O Lamb of God, I come, I come.

Just as I am, though tossed about
with many a conflict, many a doubt;
fightings and fears within, without,
O Lamb of God, I come, I come.

Just as I am, poor, wretched, blind;
sight, riches, healing of the mind,
yea, all I need, in thee to find,
O Lamb of God, I come, I come.

Just as I am, thou wilt receive;
wilt welcome, pardon, cleanse, relieve,
because thy promise I believe,
O Lamb of God, I come, I come.

Just as I am, thy love unknown
has broken every barrier down;
now to be thine, yea, thine alone,
O Lamb of God, I come, I come.

Just as I am, of that free love
the breadth, length, depth, and height to prove,
here for a season, then above:
O Lamb of God, I come, I come.

Shine Jesus Shine

Graham Kendrick (b. 1950)

Lord, the light of your love is shining
In the midst of the darkness, shining
Jesus, Light of the world, shine upon us
Set us free by the truth you now bring us
Shine on me, shine on me:

Shine, Jesus, shine
Fill this land with the Father's glory
Blaze, Spirit, blaze
Set our hearts on fire
Flow, river, flow
Flood the nations with grace and mercy
Send forth your word
Lord, and let there be light

Lord, I come to your awesome presence
From the shadows into your radiance
By the blood I may enter your brightness
Search me, try me, consume all my darkness
Shine on me, shine on me: *Refrain*

As we gaze on your kingly brightness
So our faces display your likeness
Ever changing from glory to glory
Mirrored here may our lives tell your story
Shine on me, shine on me: *Refrain*

Dear Lord and Father of Mankind
John Greenleaf Whittier (1807–92)

Dear Lord and Father of mankind,
forgive our foolish ways!
Re-clothe us in our rightful mind,
in purer lives thy service find,
in deeper reverence, praise.

In simple trust like theirs who heard,
beside the Syrian sea,
the gracious calling of the Lord,
let us, like them, without a word,
rise up and follow thee.

O Sabbath rest by Galilee!
O calm of hills above,
where Jesus knelt to share with thee
the silence of eternity
interpreted by love!

Drop thy still dews of quietness,
till all our strivings cease;
take from our souls the strain and stress,
and let our ordered lives confess
the beauty of thy peace.

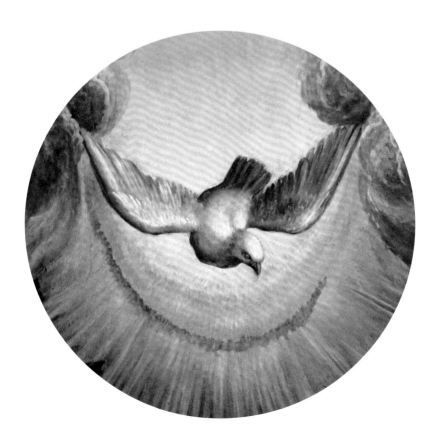

Breathe through the heats of our desire
thy coolness and thy balm;
let sense be dumb, let flesh retire;
speak through the earthquake, wind, and fire,
O still, small voice of calm.

Psalm 142
Attr. King David (c. 1040 bc–970 bc)

I call to the Lord with a loud voice;
    with loud voice I entreat his favour.
I pour out my complaint before him;
    and tell him all my trouble.
When my spirit is faint within me, you know my path;
    in the way where I walk they have hidden a snare for me.
I look to my right hand and see,
    but no man will know me.
All escape is gone,
    and there is no one who cares for me.
I call to you, O Lord, I say 'You are my refuge;
    you are my portion in the land of the living.'
Heed my loud crying, for I am brought very low.
    O save me from my persecutors,
    for they are too strong for me.
Bring me out of the prison-house,
    that I may praise your name.
When you have given me my reward,
    then will the righteous gather about me.

Before the Throne of God Above

Charitie Lees Bancroft née Smith (1841–1923)

Before the throne of God above
I have a strong, a perfect plea:
a great High Priest, whose name is Love,
who ever lives and pleads for me.

My name is graven on his hands,
my name is written on his heart;
I know that while in heaven he stands
no tongue can bid me thence depart.

When Satan tempts me to despair,
and tells me of the guilt within,
upward I look, and see him there
who made an end of all my sin.

Because the sinless Saviour died,
my sinful soul is counted free;
for God, the Just, is satisfied
to look on him and pardon me.

Behold him there! the risen Lamb!
My perfect, spotless Righteousness,
the great unchangeable I AM,
the King of glory and of grace!

One with himself, I cannot die;

my soul is purchased by his blood;

my life is hid with Christ on high,

with Christ, my Saviour and my God.

Evening Hymn
George MacDonald (1824–1905)

O God, whose daylight leadeth down
Into the sunless way,
Who with restoring sleep dost crown
The labour of the day!

What I have done, Lord, make it clean
With thy forgiveness dear;
That so to-day what might have been,
To-morrow may appear.

And when my thought is all astray,
Yet think thou on in me;
That with the new-born innocent day
My soul rise fresh and free.

Nor let me wander all in vain
Through dreams that mock and flee;
But even in visions of the brain,
Go wandering toward thee.

Be Thou My Vision

Trans. Mary Byrne (1880–1931);
versified by Eleanor Hull (1860–1935)

Be thou my vision, O Lord of my heart,
be all else but naught to me, save that thou art;
be thou my best thought in the day and the night,
both waking and sleeping, thy presence my light.

Be thou my wisdom, be thou my true word,
be thou ever with me, and I with thee Lord;
be thou my great Father, and I thy true son;
be thou in me dwelling, and I with thee one.

Be thou my breastplate, my sword for the fight;
be thou my whole armour, be thou my true might;
be thou my soul's shelter, be thou my strong tower:
O raise thou me heavenward, great Power of my power.

Riches I heed not, nor man's empty praise:
be thou mine inheritance now and always;
be thou and thou only the first in my heart;
O Sovereign of heaven, my treasure thou art.

High King of heaven, thou heaven's bright sun,
O grant me its joys after victory is won;
great Heart of my own heart, whatever befall,
still be thou my vision, O Ruler of all.

Courage & Comfort

He Sendeth Sun, He Sendeth Shower
Sarah Flower Adams (1805–48)

He sendeth sun, He sendeth shower,
Alike they're needful for the flower;
And joys and tears alike are sent
To give the soul fit nourishment.
As comes to me or cloud or sun,
Father! Thy will, not mine, be done.

Can loving children e'er reprove
With murmurs, whom they trust and love?
Creator! I would ever be
A trusting, loving child to Thee:
As comes to me or cloud or sun,
Father! Thy will, not mine, be done.

O! ne'er will I at life repine –
Enough that Thou hast made it mine.
When falls the shadow cold of death,
I yet will sing with parting breath,
As comes to me or shade or sun,
Father! Thy will, not mine, be done.

Psalm 121

I lift up my eyes to the hills:
  but where shall I find help?
My help comes from the Lord,
  who has made heaven and earth.
He will not suffer your foot to stumble,
  and he who watches over you will not sleep.
Be sure he who has charge of Israel
  will neither slumber nor sleep.
The Lord himself is your keeper;
  the Lord is your defence upon your right hand;
The sun shall not strike you by day,
  nor shall the moon by night.
The Lord will defend you from all evil;
  it is he who will guard your life.
The Lord will defend your going out and your coming in,
  from this time forward for evermore.

In Heavenly Love Abiding

Anna Laetitia Waring (1823–1910)

In heavenly love abiding,
no change my heart shall fear.
And safe in such confiding,
for nothing changes here.
The storm may roar without me,
my heart may low be laid,
but God is round about me,
and can I be dismayed?

Wherever he may guide me,
no want shall turn me back.
My Shepherd is beside me,
and nothing can I lack.
His wisdom ever waking,
his sight is never dim.
He knows the way He's taking,
and I will walk with Him.

Green pastures are before me,
which yet I have not seen.
Bright skies will soon be over me,
where darkest clouds have been.
My hope I cannot measure,
my path to life is free.
My Saviour has my treasure,
and he will walk with me.

We Rest on Thee
Edith G. Cherry (1872–97)

We rest on Thee, our Shield and our Defender!
We go not forth alone against the foe;
Strong in Thy strength, safe in Thy keeping tender,
We rest on Thee, and in Thy Name we go.
Strong in Thy strength, safe in Thy keeping tender,
We rest on Thee, and in Thy Name we go.

Yes, in Thy Name, O Captain of salvation!
In Thy dear Name, all other names above;
Jesus our Righteousness, our sure Foundation,
Our Prince of glory and our King of love.
Jesus our Righteousness, our sure Foundation,
Our Prince of glory and our King of love.

We go in faith, our own great weakness feeling,
And needing more each day Thy grace to know:
Yet from our hearts a song of triumph pealing,
'We rest on Thee, and in Thy Name we go.'
Yet from our hearts a song of triumph pealing,
'We rest on Thee, and in Thy Name we go.'

We rest on Thee, our Shield and our Defender!
Thine is the battle, Thine shall be the praise;
When passing through the gates of pearly splendour,
Victors, we rest with Thee, through endless days.
When passing through the gates of pearly splendour,
Victors, we rest with Thee, through endless days.

Psalm 46: 1-3

God is our refuge and strength,
  a very present help in trouble.
Therefore we will not fear, though the earth be moved
  and though the mountains are shaken in the midst of the sea;
Though the waters rage and foam
  and though the mountains quake at the rising of the sea.

O God Our Help in Ages Past

Isaac Watts (1674–1748)

O God, our help in ages past,
our hope for years to come,
our shelter from the stormy blast,
and our eternal home.

Under the shadow of thy throne,
thy saints have dwelt secure;
sufficient is thine arm alone,
and our defence is sure.

Before the hills in order stood,
or earth received her frame,
from everlasting thou art God,
to endless years the same.

A thousand ages in thy sight
are like an evening gone;
short as the watch that ends the night
before the rising sun.

Time, like an ever-rolling stream,
bears all its sons away;
they fly, forgotten, as a dream
dies at the opening day.

O God, our help in ages past,
our hope for years to come,
be thou our guide while troubles last,
and our eternal home!

How Firm a Foundation
Attributed to 'K'

How firm a foundation, ye saints of the Lord,
is laid for your faith in his excellent word!
What more can he say than to you he hath said,
to you that for refuge to Jesus have fled?

'Fear not, I am with thee; O be not dismayed!
For I am thy God, and will still give thee aid;
I'll strengthen thee, help thee, and cause thee to stand,
upheld by my righteous, omnipotent hand.

'When through the deep waters I call thee to go,
the rivers of woe shall not thee overflow;
for I will be with thee, thy troubles to bless,
and sanctify to thee thy deepest distress.

'When through fiery trials thy pathway shall lie,
my grace, all sufficient, shall be thy supply;
the flame shall not hurt thee; I only design
thy dross to consume, and thy gold to refine.

'The soul that on Jesus hath leaned for repose,
I will not, I will not desert to its foes;
that soul, though all hell shall endeavour to shake,
I'll never, no, never, no, never forsake.'

Will Your Anchor Hold in the Storms of Life

Priscilla Jane Owens (1829–1907)

Will your anchor hold in the storms of life,
when the clouds unfold their wings of strife?
When the strong tides lift, and the cables strain,
will your anchor drift, or firm remain?

We have an anchor that keeps the soul
steadfast and sure while the billows roll;
fastened to the Rock which cannot move,
grounded firm and deep in the Saviour's love!

Will your anchor hold in the straits of fear,
when the breakers roar and the reef is near?
While the surges rave, and the wild winds blow,
shall the angry waves then your bark o'erflow? *Refrain*

Will your anchor hold in the floods of death,
when the waters cold chill your latest breath?
On the rising tide you can never fail,
while your anchor holds within the veil. *Refrain*

Will your eyes behold through the morning light
the city of gold and the harbour bright?
Will you anchor safe by the heavenly shore,
when life's storms are past for evermore? *Refrain*

Psalm 27:1-3, 13-14
Attr. King David (c. 1040 bc—970 bc)

The Lord is my light and my salvation;
   whom then shall I fear?
   the Lord is the stronghold of my life;
   of whom shall I be afraid?
When the wicked, even my enemies and my foes,
   come upon me to devour me
   they shall stumble and fall.
If an army encamp against me, my heart shall not be afraid,
   and if war should rise against me, yet will I trust.

I believe that I shall surely see the goodness of the Lord
   in the land of the living.
O wait for the Lord;
   stand firm and he will strengthen your heart
   and wait, I say, for the Lord.

Psalm 62:1-8
Attr. King David (c. 1040 bc–970 bc)

My soul waits in silence for God,
  for from him comes my salvation.
He only is my rock and my salvation,
  my strong tower, so that I shall never be moved.
How long will you all plot against a man to destroy him,
  as though he were a leaning fence or a buckling wall?
Their design is to thrust him from his height,
  and their delight is in lies;
  they bless with their lips, but inwardly they curse.
Nevertheless, my soul, wait in silence for God,
  for from him comes my hope.
He only is my rock and my salvation,
  my strong tower, so that I shall not be moved.
In God is my deliverance and my glory;
  God is my strong rock and my shelter.
Trust in him at all times, O my people,
  pour out your hearts before him, for God is our refuge.

Be Still, My Soul

Katharina Amalia Dorothea von Schlegel (1697–1768);
trans. Jane Laurie Borthwick (1813–97)

Be still, my soul: the Lord is on thy side;
bear patiently the cross of grief or pain;
leave to thy God to order and provide;
in every change he faithful will remain.
Be still, my soul: thy best, thy heavenly Friend
through thorny ways leads to a joyful end.

Be still, my soul: thy God doth undertake
to guide the future as he has the past.
Thy hope, thy confidence let nothing shake;
all now mysterious shall be bright at last.
Be still, my soul: the waves and winds still know
his voice who ruled them while he dwelt below.

Be still, my soul: when dearest friends depart,
and all is darkened in the vale of tears,
then shalt thou better know his love, his heart,
who comes to soothe thy sorrow and thy fears.
Be still, my soul: thy Jesus can repay,
from his own fullness, all he takes away.

Be still, my soul: the hour is hastening on
when we shall be forever with the Lord,
when disappointment, grief and fear are gone,
sorrow forgot, love's purest joys restored.
Be still, my soul: when change and tears are past,
all safe and blessèd we shall meet at last.

God Moves in a Mysterious Way
William Cowper (1731–1800)

God moves in a mysterious way
his wonders to perform:
he plants his footsteps in the sea,
and rides upon the storm.

Deep in unfathomable mines,
with never-failing skill,
he treasures up his bright designs,
and works his sovereign will.

Ye fearful saints, fresh courage take;
the clouds ye so much dread
are big with mercy, and shall break
in blessings on your head.

Judge not the Lord by feeble sense,
but trust him for his grace;
behind a frowning providence
he hides a smiling face.

His purposes will ripen fast,
unfolding every hour:
the bud may have a bitter taste,
but sweet will be the flower.

Blind unbelief is sure to err,
and scan his work in vain;
God is his own interpreter,
and he will make it plain.

Abide with Me
Henry Francis Lyte (1793–1847)

Abide with me: fast falls the eventide;
the darkness deepens; Lord, with me abide:
when other helpers fail and comforts flee,
help of the helpless, O abide with me.

I need thy presence every passing hour;
what but thy grace can foil the tempter's power?
Who, like thyself, my guide and stay can be?
Through cloud and sunshine, Lord, abide with me.

I fear no foe, with thee at hand to bless;
ills have no weight, and tears no bitterness.
Where is death's dark sting? where, grave, thy victory?
I triumph still, if thou abide with me.

Hold thou thy cross before my closing eyes;
shine through the gloom, and point me to the skies;
heaven's morning breaks, and earth's vain shadows flee;
in life, in death, O Lord, abide with me.

Oft in Danger, Oft in Woe

Henry Kirke White (1785–1806); added to by
Frances Sara Fuller-Maitland (1809–77)

Oft in danger, oft in woe,
onward, Christian, onward go:
bear the toil, maintain the strife,
strengthened with the Bread of Life.

Onward Christians, onward go,
join the war and face the foe;
will ye flee in danger's hour?
Know ye not your Captain's power?

Let your drooping hearts be glad:
march in heavenly armor clad:
fight, nor think the battle long,
victory soon shall be your song.

Let not sorrow dim your eye,
soon shall every tear be dry;
let not fears your course impede,
great your strength, if great your need.

Onward then in battle move,
more than conquerors ye shall prove;
though opposed by many a foe,
Christian soldiers, onward go.

Nearer My God, to Thee
Sarah Flower Adams (1805–48)

Nearer, my God, to thee, nearer to thee!
E'en though it be a cross that raiseth me,
still all my song shall be, nearer, my God, to thee.

Nearer, my God, to thee,
nearer to thee!

Though like the wanderer, the sun gone down,
darkness be over me, my rest a stone.
yet in my dreams I'd be nearer, my God to thee. *Refrain*

There let the way appear, steps unto heav'n;
all that thou sendest me, in mercy given;
angels to beckon me nearer, my God, to thee. *Refrain*

Then, with my waking thoughts bright with thy praise,
out of my stony griefs Bethel I'll raise;
so by my woes to be nearer, my God, to thee. *Refrain*

Or, if on joyful wing cleaving the sky,
sun, moon, and stars forgot, upward I'll fly,
still all my song shall be, nearer, my God, to thee. *Refrain*

There in my Father's home, safe and at rest,
there in my Saviour's love, perfectly blest;
age after age to be, nearer my God to thee. *Refrain*

Fight the Good Fight
John Samuel Bewley Monsell, Jr. (1811–75)

Fight the good fight with all thy might,
Christ is thy strength and Christ thy right;
lay hold on life, and it shall be
thy joy and crown eternally.

Run the straight race, through God's good grace,
lift up thine eyes and seek his face;
life with its way before us lies,
Christ is the path and Christ the prize.

Cast care aside, lean on thy Guide;
his boundless mercy will provide;
trust, and thy trusting soul shall prove
Christ is its life and Christ its love.

Faint not nor fear, his arms are near;
he changeth not, and thou art dear;
only believe, and thou shalt see
that Christ is all in all to thee.

Awake Our Souls, Away Our Fears
Isaac Watts (1674–1748)

Awake, our souls! away, our fears!
Let every trembling thought be gone!
Awake, and run the heavenly race,
And put a cheerful courage on.

True, 'tis a strait and thorny road,
And mortal spirits tire and faint;
But they forget the mighty God,
That feeds the strength of every saint.

O mighty God, Thy matchless power
Is ever new, and ever young;
And firm endures, while endless years
Their everlasting circles run.

From Thee, the ever flowing spring,
Our souls shall drink a fresh supply;
While such as trust their native strength
Shall melt away, and droop, and die.

Swift as the eagle cuts the air,
We'll mount aloft to Thine abode;
On wings of love our souls shall fly,
Nor tire along the heavenly road.

Picture Credits & Acknowledgments

1 & 61   Edward John Poynter (1836-1919), *Music, Heavenly Maid*, © Christie's Images Ltd./SuperStock

3 & 31   Charles Chaplin (1825-91), *Girl with Doves*, © Christie's Images Ltd./SuperStock

4   Sir Frank Dicksee (1853-1928), *Ophelia*, © Fine Art Images/SuperStock

7   Bernhard Plockhorst (1825-1907), *The Good Shepherd*, © SuperStock

9   Johann Friedrich Overbeck (1789-1869), *The Holy Family*, © SuperStock

10-11   Abbott Fuller Graves (1859-1936), *Bouquet of Roses* , © Christie's Images/SuperStock

13   Marie Spartali Stillman (1844-1927), *Fiammetta Singing*, © Christie's Images Ltd./SuperStock

14   Charles Courtney Curran (1861-1942), *On the Heights*, Wikimedia Commons/Brooklyn Museum/KenjiMizoguchi

17   Joseph Martin Kronheim (1810-96), *Christian Loses His Burden at the Cross* (Colour plate from *The Pilgrim's Progress* by John Bunyan, 1628-88), © Universal Images Group/SuperStock

19   Caspar David Friedrich (1774-1840), *Two Men Contemplating the Moon*, Wikimedia Commons/Sebastian Nizan

23   Constantin Hansen (1804-80), *The Resurrection*, © SuperStock

26-27   Albert Bierstadt (1830-1902), *Among the Sierra Nevada, California*, Wikimedia Commons/Paris 16

32   William-Adolphe Bouguereau (1825-1905), *Song of the Angels*, © Creative Commons/leo.jeje

35   Bartolomé Esteban Murillo (1617-82), *Assumption of the Virgin*, © Bridgeman Art Library, London/SuperStock

37   Paul Wagner (1852-1937), *The Iris Beauty*, © Christie's Images Ltd./SuperStock

39   Thomas Moran (1837-1926), *Mountain of the Holy Cross*, © SuperStock

40   Angelica Kauffman (1741-1807), *Portrait of a Woman Dressed as a Vestal Virgin*, courtesy of The Yorck Project and © Dresden Old Masters Gallery

43   Bartolomé Esteban Murillo (1617-82), *The Christ Child as Shepherd*, © SuperStock

45   László Mednyánszky (1852-1919), *Frosty Forest (Windy Dawn)*, Wikimedia Commons/Szilas

47   Thomas Sully (1783-1872), *Lady Carrying Holly Branches*, © Christie's Images Ltd./SuperStock

48-49   Thomas Cole (1801-48), *Cross at Sunset*, © Creative Commons/Daderot

51   Dante Gabriel Rossetti (1828-82), *Beata Beatrix*, © World History Archive/SuperStock

53   Gabriel Ferrier (1847-1914) , *The Guardian Angel*, © Fine Art Photographic Library/SuperStock

54   Ivan Shishkin (1832-98), *In the Park*, Wikimedia Commons/Anagoria

57   Émile Vernon (1872-1919), *A Sweet Glance*, Wikimedia Commons/FA2010

59   William Holman Hunt (1827-1910), *The Light of the World*, © SuperStock

63   Thomas Cole (1801-48), *The Voyage of Life: Old Age*, © ACME Imagery/SuperStock

65   Claude Monet (1840-1926), *Woman with a Parasol – Madame Monet and Her Son*, National Gallery of Art, Washington DC, USA/Photo © AISA/The Bridgeman Art Library

67   James Tissot (1836-1902), *The Voice of the Lord*, © SuperStock

70-71   Frederic Edwin Church (1826-1900), *Cross in the Wilderness*, © Creative Commons/Daderot

75   Henry Courtney Selous (1803-90), Illustration for an 1844 edition of *The Pilgrim's Progress* by John Bunyan (1628-88), © World History Archive/SuperStock

76   Henri Biva (1848-1929), *Poppies*, © Fine Art Photographic Library/SuperStock

79   Jacob Jordaens (1593-1678), detail from *The Adoration of the Shepherds*, © SuperStock

81   Caspar David Friedrich (1774-1840), *Ulrich von Hutten's Grave*, Wikimedia Commons/Hajotthu

83   Philippe de Champaigne (1602-74), *The Good Shepherd*, © SuperStock

86-87   Jean-François Millet (1814-75), *The Angelus*, courtesy of Google Cultural Institute and © Musée d'Orsay

89   Alexander Koester (1864-1932), *Five Ducks on the River, Stony Shore*, © Christie's Images Ltd./SuperStock

90   Carlo Dolci (1616-86), *Christ in the Garden of Gethsemane*, © Universal Images Group/SuperStock

93   Thomas Cole (1801-48), *Mountain Sunrise, Catskill*, Wikimedia Commons/Cobalty

All psalms and extracts from psalms courtesy of oremus.org and *The Liturgical Psalter* © 1976, 1977, David L. Frost, John A. Emerton, Andrew A. Macintosh.

With thanks for permission to reproduce the following hymns:
I Danced in the Morning (Lord of the Dance) (p84): © 1963 Stainer & Bell Ltd, 23 Gruneisen Road, London N3 1DZ, England. *www.stainer.co.uk*. Used by permission.
Shine Jesus Shine (p108): Graham Kendrick © 1987 Make Way Music. *www.grahamkendrick.co.uk*
Be Still for the Presence of the Lord (p20): © 1986 Thankyou Music (Adm. by *CapitolCMGPublishing.com* excl. UK & Europe, adm. by Integrity Music, part of the David C Cook family, *songs@integritymusic.com*)
How Great Thou Art (p22): © 1949 and 1953 by the Stuart Hine Trust. All rights in the USA its territories and possessions, except print rights, administered by Capitol CMG Publishing. USA, North, Central and South America print rights administered by Hope Publishing Company. All other non US Americas rights administered by the Stuart Hine Trust. Rest of the world rights administered by Integrity Music Europe, part of the David C Cook family, *songs@integritymusic.com*

Index of Titles

Index of Authors